This Business of Wisdom

This Business of Wisdom

Lauren Camp

Santa Fe, NM
August 2022

The author wishes to thank the editors of the following publications for first acknowledging a number of the poems (sometimes in earlier versions) that appear in this manuscript:

The Comstock Review

Cradle Songs: An Anthology on Motherhood
(Quill and Parchment Press)

The Mountains Have Made Us Anthology
(Southwest Literary Center)

Rhino

Santa Fe Literary Review

The Sow's Ear Poetry Review

Thema

Upstairs at Duroc

Wild Goose Poetry Review

This Business of Wisdom
Copyright © 2010 by Lauren Camp. All rights reserved.

Printed in the United States of America
First edition: September 2010
ISBN 978-0-9826968-2-8

Book design by David Camp • www.thesoundatreemakes.com

Cover art: *Earth Drawing III* (detail) by Lauren Camp
www.laurencamp.com

Published by West End Press • www.westendpress.org

This Business of Wisdom is the seventh volume in the West End Press New Series, featuring full-length titles by emerging and recently recognized authors.

West End Press is a registered 501(c)3 non-profit organization that relies on public support to publish "voices from the margins." Financial contributions are welcome and are tax-deductible.

to David, everything that is

Contents

One

The Magic of Seeing

Notice the yellowing tape
and the graphite hatches scattered across the paper:
a dark diagram

of saved details. Notice the pattern
scored into each layer,
then stripped and curved away, the long arc

of sunlit days gilded into squares.
Toss your small goodbyes into the sanded planes
and the grid

slumped into a vague halo of wax. Notice the spaces
for your worries. Notice
the buoyant red and its authority

over the canvas, the way it seems to be igniting.
Notice lines that have collapsed, the ripped
and wrung-out corners

and the ruthless ones,
each a departure from perfect balance. Notice the sweat,
the swagger of trees, the shadow, and the scale.

You stand in a pinhole, surfacing again in a haze
of light – a paradox of vision; this is the view
from the constructed earth, the sea,

the future. You are folded into the shape
and stretch; your sure eye
will see the ghosts, the yeasty texture of deliberation

caked on and scraped off. Concentrate on the bruises:
the pauses –
and the breaks, each quarrel

of pigment, the devotion to luck
and the points of harmony, the drips, the gin,
the risk

and negative space; enjoy the language
of the hand and the small stroke of reason.
A shy ripple haunts the tall gray letters; notice

the horses' hooves, the fruit bowl, the spattered bloom
of bravery, the virtue of the varnish.
Listen to the slashes, the fire.

Notice the dots. And those
repeating orange cars. And when your hands ask,
love the hands that built this, that tilted back the paint

into blades and eyes.
Notice the white, the thunderous white
brooding with invisible butterflies in the center of the picture.

Lovebirds

I drive home to find
dove feathers

embossed on the plate glass
on the cheek of the house.

I sit
on the loose step

of the porch rocking back
and forth under the green-

leafed sky.
I didn't see

the two birds
who flew whole

and ecstatic
into the dazzling light

leaving only an outline
of their twinned bodies.

It takes a willing partner
to trade sun

for a sheet
of heaven as fast as that.

To my man I said
nothing

about attraction
but minutes later

we watched two
roadrunners jumping

on the breeze
of Love's crazy spells.

In these cantankerous days
we must find ways

to fling ourselves
into the right wounded world

opening doors of sky
inward and outward.

The House on Theresa Lane

This place is a cathedral. An aria in an endless open space.

Here is where the UPS truck turns,
and where the driver once bashed the basin
of the cottonwood tree we put in eight years ago.
And this is the porch and my front door
where he left a note of apology.

My front door, a good wood but I couldn't
tell you which; I know my woods fairly well:
walnut, cherry, oak, sometimes ash and poplar.
I learned when I lived out west. Learned
as my husband made sawdust from his boards.

I learned birds here at the kitchen table:
towhees and robins, finches, blue jays, flickers.
This afternoon, I saw a black-hooded grosbeak
and a spotted roadrunner.

We brought the table from California.
This is our meeting ground, where we talk,
a place for dinner. In the front, two drawers
to hold my gentility (cloth napkins, bamboo mats)
and my imagination (paper, pens, clips).

We are in my kitchen now, with the open shelves.
Black ceramic plates I bought in Chinatown,
a serving for six. I've never used them all.
These are the plates I wash and put away.

We don't break many dishes, even when someone
is angry. I might hold a cup in my hand and the chaos
inside will make me want to throw it,
but instead I shake my hands in space
as though the air bothers me.

This is the hole in my bedroom.
If you sit on the floor, you can see it clearly.
We must have been sitting there. He was angry
and he punched the wall.
I always see that indentation when I come in here to sleep.

The Soup Aisle at Trader Joe's

Wednesday night: we have come in for two cans
of onion soup. I am studying the seasoned nuts, the chips.
I have looked away and when I return my attention to him,
he has spilled onto the hard ground, his flesh relaxed
but bent up into a riddle of bones on a bed of tile,
his blue eyes open and empty below the sparkle
of reflective tin and loose people jangling like coins
around us. I step over the folded angles of his rubber limbs,
lullaby his face with frightened fingertips. I am hovering,
a foolish sense that if I whisper in perfect syllables,
he will bloom again. I am cold and he is not breathing.
Help is missing everywhere; they bring water but
his mouth is slack. A minute lasts an hour
and I need to figure out how I will understand
his filing system, where he stores the lightbulbs.
Why I ever laughed before. But, as I am considering,
the suspended night, winter-hinged and pulsing,
reaches in and straightens him. The man with a deep scar
sings the hot low sound of human. His joints moan
as bruises form, dark and salty on his skin.

Apple Wine

I want to touch grass, to crawl into daylight slowly,
limbs emptying into each grain of sand,

want to seed my body into the earth
until autumn rises, pick tomatoes,

peel the thin layer of promise to a center.
Behind me, I want you:

a handful of smoke,
a garden that whispers, a broken glass, my pulse.

Do you remember the apple wine?
Twelve sips, someone else's yard.

I could wander forever,
turning the forgotten taste of sour green on my tongue.

This Morning a Wasp's Nest

This morning a wasp's nest kept me from my breakfast,
a nest the size of a fist, or a small heart, chambered and dark,
growing stingers stuck to the shadow of the porch near the door.

My narrow definition of today did not include this time
to study the holes the velvet ants are filling with their bodies,
or their new wings planted in the jail-space of each small cell.
But now I want to see each tiny hair on their thorax and abdomens,

their compound eyes, and hear the long dry bread of their silent breathing.
Sometime this spring while I was in the garden, the queen's spit mixed
with the edges of my plants to form a dull brown cradle for the eggs.

Here it is September and I was tormented by the summer
streaking past my window, unable to stop watching the remnant
of what was left: the jackrabbits, lizards, the hummingbirds.

This colony, maybe several thousand growing paper wasps,
and my stomach is broken and shuddering, but every day I will have to look,
to enter the rising cold to watch the sweet secretions
and the growing umbrella of their combs.

One day when I open the door, the rose-pink globe of earth
will be washed with the new wasps, their jointed bodies
entering the air in a sudden arc. I wonder

if I will be able to do the things I have decided to do that day, or
if I will have to sit on the porch in my winter coat and slippers,
waving them off as they leave.

Woman Kept Captive for 24 Years

Whatever they tell me on the news this time,
I will see three children raisined in the dark
between the basement and the old man. I will hear
the mother's eyes lock down with each unwanted entry,
each night passing through a boundary
of shame, each night swallowing the same wrong
as her father splays the petals between her legs
with his body. Her eyes will shut hard,
closing over the black ruin of her flesh,
and her smile will leak hope. At 42, she is buried
beneath eight locks, hidden
from the sun, folding missing time like an answer
into years. The story repeated six times
this morning, and whatever attention I give it
feels as if I've rotted inside, as if the wild
pollen of my own love will pour out of my body,
dark and bitter, naked and ashamed. A basement!
such a silent haunted place to plant a family.
Home is never false, never clean. Her children
will perfect their childhood, bending
promises like broken birds into the landscape
of their small selves, washing
in the only invisible strip of untouched light.
The mother keeps unwrapping edges and listens
to herself get older. She is news
and I am innocent, stepping off the curb
into my life, and wavering.

---

*Austrian police have arrested a 73-year-old man believed to have
imprisoned his daughter in a windowless basement for 24 years. The
woman told police she gave birth to seven children after being repeatedly
raped by her father during her captivity.*

– Associated Press, April 28, 2008

To the Father Whose Five Girls
Were Killed in Their Bed

How old were they, your girls?
Each one a world, growing into its fields and oceans,

the zigzag of their brown hair
on the pillow, and fingers twisted

between them as they slept
together, in the same bed, passing dreams

into dark, the calm white buds of them.
Oh, your wounded eyes, your screaming;

you will live in the hollow of their room
with the fur of their photos, your heart

in flight, already fighting
the liquid shape of greed,

a spark of madness tight-knotted to your future.
Let go of memory and reason.

It is true you will not sing again
but do not rise from this thing of pain

hurling defeat beyond long ghetto lines
into the families who scarred you.

Others can read your closed face
on every fat day, every too-

bright sun and every silence.
Leaves still cleave to the trees in spring.

That night came on in shades of cinnamon
and tamarind; they were asleep, your girls.

The familiar shape of their small bodies,
let that shape emboss your body, your fingers,

imprint each hair on your breast.
They were asleep, and now you must awaken

into the long angles of the blood-glint sky.
No electricity but the frightening light of loss.

Tell me everything you know
about your girls. Tell me everything,

and then tell me again.
Tell me the burden of your wife's bearing

of them, how each head crowned, their first cries.
Their innocence will answer.

They left without warning, without
the pinprick of leaving.

Let them become maps and tears
on the broken bridge of your memory,

but oh, their skin, the flower-sweet scent of their skin!
Remember that, in your short history of love.

Israeli air raids have pounded the Gaza Strip for a third day, hitting key sites linked to militant group Hamas.

– BBC News, December 29, 2008

An Israeli bomb struck the refugee camp's Imad Aqil mosque around midnight... The force of the blast was so massive it also brought down the Balousha family's house, which yesterday lay in ruins. The seven eldest girls were asleep together on mattresses in one bedroom and they bore the brunt of the explosion.

– Guardian News, December 29, 2008

Fundamental Science

One – Megumi Yamamoto, UNM Doctoral Student

In physics class she considers each hypothesis
then travels to the mountain with her lover.
Lake Katherine drowses while
they climb the equation of the apex.
Megumi is responding to the little world,
the wild penstemon and ivy leaf,
when the wind unrolls with force
and a storm comes hiking past,
arriving late from the edge of nowhere.
Megumi touches her lover's forehead;
he smoothes her straight, black hair.
Cold air wraps and separates,
creases a dividing line between them.
When Megumi reaches out,
her lover has disappeared.
The word *goodbye* becomes a prayer.
She crystallizes absence into numbers
on a cell phone; dials 9-1-1.

Two - Sgt. Andy Tingwall, Chief Pilot

The copter collides with a thicket of frost
before it finds a woman with long, dark hair.
The pilot gathers her,
and the spotter secures the door.
When the craft ascends, sky reorganizes,
pushing its hands over them in a whirl
of black gestures. A torment drags the engine,
sketching loud lines on straining air.
Sky becomes nonexistent. Tingwall probes,
nosing blindly toward the summit,
rigorously pitching into clouds,
but the tail rotor hits a tree and spins.

Surrounded by small ghosts of altitude,
the aircraft rubs against the impossible beast
of wind. Wind dives into it,
again and again, hungry and clutching,
tugging at its attachment
to aimless molecules of air: the droning
path of wind, a lullaby
of wind. Tingwall raises the machine
into hurling shadows of energy and matter.
He cries once as the copter wracks the mountain
then torques and skids, its open eye
fastened on the approaching spine of earth.

Three - Wesley Cox, Spotter

A copter, after all, is only metal and motor.
We tried to center it, to keep Megumi safe,
but the wind protested
and the girl was broken when we three tossed out,
her dark hair spread on tender snow.
I was wrapped in fuselage; Andy out of sight.
The universe closed.
An unwieldy air raked through us as we called
the broken angles of our names,
our voices casting about
in the glossy landscape for each other.
What caught my ear was *Wes*,
and when my name stopped coming,
when the wind rose once more
with its compulsive shuddering, I understood
the physics of what had happened.

---

*In June 2009, pilot Sgt. Andy Tingwall was killed in a search and
rescue mission on Santa Fe Baldy as he tried to save lost hiker and
UNM graduate physics student Megumi Yamamoto, who was also
killed in the freak summer blizzard. Tactical Flight Officer Wesley
Cox survived the crash.*

The Need to Punctuate

After Monday's news, I keep hearing:
Nigerians cut down with machetes in religious massacre!
Half million people pushed from ancestral homes in the Rwenzori Mountains!
Hundreds subsumed by mudslides in eastern Uganda!
Bloody narcomafia shootings through Murder City, Juarez!
Massive quake and torrents of rain rip Chile apart!
Tsunami advisory for the Big Island!

I tell my students that their stories must run in a straight line.
Punctuation is the road map we follow.
Battle over the blade and hook of each comma.
Drop periods into each long corridor of words.
Land precisely on one side of the sentence,
– and capitalize. With intention.

But don't exclaim unless it is remarkable, we tutors say:
    to Connie, outlining research paper #3, for English 109,
        on the Navajo Code Talkers
        who saved the U.S. in the Second World War,
    to Karen, polishing a four-pager on Borges' 'Gospel
        According to Mark,' in which 33-year-old, bearded Espinosa
        will die on a homemade cross,
    or to Jake, whose paper about the tingle and dread of finding his father
        after 24 ruined years in jail
        (for something he doesn't mention) earns him a B minus,
    and to Hadley, 43, with a streak of silver and freckles, a slippery smile,
        and a fourth draft of her personal narrative on McAuley Manor,
        a nun-run house for six teenagers
        saved from existing at the abandoned edges of their parents.

Do not use exclamation points, we say. *Tell it as it is.*

Rings
(for Eric Dolphy, 1964)

On a ledge, I align 20 stones,
dark ovals smooth as the inside of my thigh, small orbs

ringed with white.
"Something Sweet, Something Tender,"

circles written when the seas retreated,
the raw song of mourning.

Dolphy's clarinet turns a slow tide that surges and drifts.
He holds a bag of logic and many colors

fitted into keys, an anthem of sense and anger,
the loud shadow of a burden. His reed pushes, scatters.

Vibes burble on the ocean of tomorrow
as bass strings sink spasms

of plodding sadness in cool air; each returning swell
a sphere collected on a beach the size of sound.

The trumpet comes in sullen; tones drop
like an anchor.

No one realizes, and a soul bleeds.
New language forms.

Everyone collects behind the beat
until the clarinet grabs a line and knots up dusk

with ginger-sharp thought.
Understanding makes me dizzy. My pulse syncopates

in rhythm to the plucked, torn sound,
a noise that wears itself down, the chunked voice

of five men playing a deep confusion layered by time,
the sediment constantly smoothing, forever softening,

until all that remains is dark –
rimmed with a white bracelet from another era.

Satchmo's Mouth

Satchmo I said
                        can I crawl
            inside your mouth
                  the temple, the *tempo*

of grunting sunlight
                dry gravel self
                    against self
        the gritty timbre of time

            you are
my confession I worship
        the bright windows of your teeth
opening into

                fading to forgiveness
feed me grass and ice cream
                the wisdom
            of the messy world

but I was dreaming
          a chord   of velvet kisses
           the jute-skinned nap
rapid revolutions of parched sound

A Hum

Charles Mingus
                              hums anger
              notes that curve and pitch
                     across the room
a sound that stretches out like wings

              I hear him wade
in black fury gospel
                         a fistful
of dark trees emerging from his heart

each note somersaults
              prickly at times or funk whirl tilted
       and returns mercy drenched

       the bass breaks with a loud splinter
and the humming starts again

call it religion   or worship

a buzz of sharp light
       becomes scales and chords
                            his scalding body

                 and his humming head

       the drone of piss poor hope
his bellow rift
              deep   his shadow thrumming
                            angling into traffic

each tone a record of revelation
                 the murmur of dissent and echo
          puzzling itself
                            into fervent

19

At a Concert of Experimental Music

To keep everything is to be defeated;
we listen to the band quiver –
all squawk, no sinew in those high-pitched tones
arguing
for margins;
we are intoxicated
as instruments speak their disfigured parables; we listen
at a threshold of screeches;
our bodies become inlets, a chart
of sound that is rough rocks and slanted bridges;
we inhabit the tight landscape of energy;
we fill seashells with sound and it becomes sense,
but we let it go again –
until the next tune tunnels through us.

Two

My First Year

In 1967, my mother is already my mother
in the seedy boiled metal of Manhattan
below the women's fancy clothing at Macy's Herald Square

where she works and buys her clothes.
In 1967, my mother has stopped her cigarettes;
the U.S. blasts through Operations Latchkey and Crosstie

with tests named Bourbon, Persimmon,
Fizz, Cerise and Polka
(apt descriptions of my mother's vibrant outfits),

and my little wrinkled body stretches out.
My father bathes my hot pink flesh in a plastic tub.
John and Paul sing Penny Lane.

We wander to the park at 4th and Waverly,
my mother in coral bell-bottoms and a yellow blouse.
Returning home she sips rosé,

satisfied. In 1967, NBC argues the Vietnam War,
a frenzy of race riots. My parents, too busy to listen.
What they don't hear keeps climbing away.

My father watches the first Super Bowl as a married man.
Peggy Fleming skates in a formal ice rink dressed in pink,
my mother's eyes entranced.

My mother buys a charming pea coat for her 5'10" frame.
Sex oozes onto streets and down alleys.
Neil Armstrong practices landing on the moon.

In 1967, everyone drops acid while my father goes to work.
From the couch, my parents watch Milton Berle.
My mother lands in the city of humor

and stays there smiling as the show keeps ending.
In 1967, my mother drags my cradle to the TV set.
Fred Rogers walks us through the neighborhood

and my mother grits her teeth. Fred teaches make believe
while my mother organizes her pretty clothing.
What is happening isn't happening in my house.

Pinball Wizard

The pinball machine was silent
for a minute and he knew that meant
he should go next door
right then
to where his parents were pressing
clothes and remembering
the customers' shirt sizes
and names, and whether
they had spots they needed out,
but the machine was bumping
and beeping again,
and the whole room was knocking about
even as he began to walk away,
and he wanted back
into the bright lights and colors
which suited him better
than the steam and his father's
counting of dollars and
if only he had some more
change – a quarter, maybe,

in one of those endless pockets –
he would go back there again
to flip the levers
and forget the flipping fury
of his dad at the end
of the day
because it is there,
in the back of this store,
where drunks roll in
for bottles and lottery tickets
sell by the dozens
and Yodels and Suzy-Qs sit
hopeful in their cellophane,
waiting for someone with a quarter,
a dime, a hunger,
it is only there
in that dusty room
that he is loud enough
and smart enough and prepared
for the next unexpected shot.

The Model of Perfection

My sister poured over into sleep
each night, her family of dolls lined up

around her in the red room,
and when they pushed into channels

of the twin bed
with their ecstatic colors, she responded

with patience for her dolls,
never worried

about the stuffed heads
and how their brains seemed to slip out

in threads and jumbled cloth,
or about the hairline cracks in the ceramic faces

or the way limbs jointed in all directions,
twisted

and dangling. She endured
the dead-white skin

and listened as their carved, painted mouths
clamped down on their stories.

She preferred silence,
my sister. For her, it was enough

that their big heads towered over flimsy bodies.
She squeezed

her dolls into corners,
and each night as the air unzipped

with its tarnished breath in the eyeful dark,
her brown eyes looked into

glass eyes and whispered *good night*
to dozens of pursed lips.

Growing Up

We never move
from the little street, watch
the other houses, vigilant and tall.
Girls skip afternoon shadows
through looping ropes. Swings lift
and fall to a chain link fence
and a small field of crisp Italian beans.
Inside, an attic fan rumbles with no tongue,
the heavy blade pushing relentless heat,
burnishing rooms with discontent.
I store Dad's Playboys under the bed,
settled at the center,
the magazine smell slick on my fingertips
(each picture a scrambled equation for evolution
embossing the space between my legs).
I sleep upside down,
keep snakes as angry invisible pets
to provoke me in the night. I cry,
wake and tumble down stairs,
eat corn flakes while my sister spits,
her tart frown leaning on the floor;
drop my dreams at the bus stop
and collect them again each afternoon;
break my arm at an intersection,
break it again on the cusp of freedom.
Our house keeps remarking
until the night I leave. I lunge away,
stitch new angles into the first hundred days.
My parents buy a house
on the other side of town, the dark red shock
of stacked brick, the walls a scowl of white.
No one opens the front door until the day she dies.

Wisconsin

One year you mention Wisconsin, so I unearth
my Imperial Edition of Rand McNally's '68 atlas.
I run my fingers down the coast, drawing a thick line
of hopeful sweat from Sturgeon Bay to Kenosha.
I feel the west edge of Lake Michigan.
A breeze blows contentedly off the solid basin
of water on the map, sighing a shade of pastel blue into my face.

We could spend hours lazing by Fond du Lac at Lake Winnebago.
I will take pictures of you with my digital camera.
You, in those beige pants against the pure blue of the water.
Your eyes will turn down like fish, even though you are smiling.

But no, Fond du Lac is industrial and urban – not lazy.
I reach further north on the map.
What if, instead, we fly to Duluth, with its black lines and squares?
We could rent a budget car, then motor to Minnesota for Spam sandwiches.
Minnesota! Think of it – we've never been.

It will begin to get late and we'll agree to head back,
across the top fold of Wisconsin
past Cornucopia through Bad River Indian Reservation.
The rez feels moist under my dry fingers, with its miniature acres of rice.
Maybe we will see a beaver, a rabbit, a doe.
You will remind me about your trip to Second Mesa with Mom
and mention the Pilgrims, because that is what you know
of Indians. We will stop for pie and cheese
before we drive on to Hurley and Upson
and Land O'Lakes. You will, of course, buy butter.

Because we have plenty of time, we'll wander into Michigan
(to Norway and Vulcan – a shade of ruddy violet like heated iron),
then south to Marinette (green),
and we'll peer across to Egg Harbor where, I imagine,
the sun rises like a yolk
on the flat pan of the bay. I hope we get to see this, the dish of this light.
You would be calm here because water soothes you,
especially blue water. There are no waves on my map.
I would watch wrinkles break on the shore of your old face.

We will be pleased with ourselves for reaching three states,
and, even though I will never forget,
you will tell me that my mother went to school in Madison,
which is starred on page 88.
I am more interested in Baraboo
because it sounds like a thunder of elk moving through a vacuum cleaner,
and has the distinction of sitting just above N. Freedom.
If it is summer, I will gently ask if you'd like to raft
down the river of Freedom, floating along
in the mosquitoed heat.

But we won't do this. We never do things like this.
Instead, we will visit the dorms at UW.
Mom might have stayed here – or here, you'll say, as you point to each building.
But, even this we won't do. Because just when I agree
to the itinerary you want, you'll mention Branson, Missouri.

Sick

When I couldn't recover, I walked between the ash
and the echinacea, dripping water on the garden.

I straightened each stone step and created a cloud
of sparrows. The sky bandaged in the places I ached most.

I fought the battle of Okinawa; then I was Billie Holiday
shooting up. Do not be alarmed.

I ate all the soup
and walked down the dirt road of despair

to the bend where the truck slipped once
and snow drains to particles of mud.

Hours slowly darkened until night was strewn everywhere.
I entered the bed, occupying the spaces

between danger and calm, the cold sheets of sickness.
I was unable to be fully wrecked.

I landscaped my life with the small white bulb above my head
and pressed myself

into books, tidy and unhappy. I was embracing the slow anger
of the body that requires obedience, the emotion

of exhaustion. I forgave myself the tight turquoise of wanting and crept
into the quiet room of myself again, turning pages.

Looking for a doorbell
or anything to ring, I dreamt I was a house,

emptied of all its charms.

The Invisible Line of Sleep

I closed my eyes while he was talking
and saw a woman at a table
turn into another face
at that same table
and then another
and another –
so many women
becoming other women
becoming themselves
until I stopped looking
and he was still talking
and it was dark
and the table was gone

Control

She walked into 8th grade and out of 9th.

Tatjana.

Even her name sashayed into the room,
each silver bangle swaggering loosely along her arm.

She pulled up from Tuckahoe, dipped in denim.
School was a swollen throat, a yellow bus,
and spring never arrived twice.

We accumulated adolescence in a brick building
tilting forward into periods and elocution.

She weighed rules against mistakes,
ruffling through class in spandex,
all patterned with polish and liquid strokes of liner.

My best friend,
and her parents erased her from my life.
An attempted reduction of her plural, unstable self.

There was no god in that girl. I know that now;
she was skin, vessel, need, nerve,
spelling interactions from the world into her pockets.

The list of things she *owned* was always longer, always
lengthening. With each thing Tatjana stole,
she became more of something than I have ever been.

In synagogue, they taught us honor.
Every Saturday, offering adulation to a quiet god
who fixed our futures in struggle and engulfed us
in vague voyages of witness and service.

But there were twinges
as I watched Tatjana, randy from the pinching,
unperturbed by how her wild self
kept staggering about, consumed
with the bright arcade of gathering.

When I think now of my flaws of fragility,
those things I've heaved into adulthood
with such strict adherence to procedure,
I consider Tatjana, wherever she is,

furtively opening the door in, door out
into the slow cold of desperation,
brushing her hands against each blunder.

The Student

She ladles a bowl of cheese soup,
the waves of cream sloshing
golden against the rim of white,
then moves thickly to the dark
corner of the room;
she opens her textbook
but reads faces in the space
where words might be.
The soup's steam smokes up slowly,
enveloping her in a necklace
of silver filigrees.
In the busy room, nobody mentions
her name and she forgets it,
the rough sound of hard syllables
stewed together for twenty years.
She encloses her senses
in the rich paste of butter,
the bath of fatty liquid,
and the oily crumbs
left from the croutons,
then returns for another bowl.
Snow continues stepping down
from the sky in small flakes.
The student eats until the pot
is empty, until she is,
in some way, full.
When she exits the cafeteria,
her body is heavy and she hefts it,
alone, in the invisible snow.

In the Locker Room

At the gym
watching bodies come and go.
Through locker vents I spy
on pliant skin, the palpable
thickness of another woman
whose parts sway
and balance on each other
in a garbled indentation of fat.
She lifts up her generous
underwear, covers the soft wide hairs
at her center. Her humble exertions.
The bulky waves of in-out breaths.
She reaches along the total volume
of herself to tie her shoes.
That is the body I once had,
ledges instead of curves.
Years ago I obliged perfection,
flattened my folds and flaps.
Early morning weigh-ins,
an apple for lunch,
a temper tantrum of starving cells.
In weeks my body reconfigured.
I spent a decade grasping
the empty space.
What I realize is how I hold myself now,
the geography of this whispering
slender structure, the commands
and distillation of bones
that contain my life.
But I admire the other body,
the mortal aspect,
how her inside is glued right there
to the outside for everyone to notice.

Thievery

She walks in a city
made of sound,
a neighborhood
smudged and garish
with the chatter
and squawk
of human anatomy
strewn carelessly
on street corners.
She pulls petals
from gardens
as she passes,
risking a guilty chorus
of whispering pansies
as a spectrum of color
leaks steadily
from her moist palms.
The sun lies lazy
on the sidewalk

as the young woman
gathers temporary pigments
to mail to everyone
she knows.
At home, she presses
her findings flat
between *obituary*
and *ornithology*.
Stamens emboss
pages 904 to 927,
coloring a dynasty
of syllables and
parts of speech,
pronunciation,
origin and definition.
Peculated corollas crisp
while she seeds
into sleep.

Call-Back Mammogram

Her bare feet point
toward the large vein-blue appliance
in this small windowless room
where she is woven
into a cotton gown, almost puce
but with enough pure pink to be girlish,
the cloth tethered at her waist
and hanging from one shoulder.
She slopes her body forward
while the technician with rich curls
flattens her breast into the machine,
prattling about Buddhism
and the economy
as she turns the knob,
compressing the fatty tissue,
pushing her deeper
under the plastic plate,
reminding her not to breathe,
not to complain.
The angles they took last week
were clouded
and rough, their shadings
darker than the baseline
two years ago. On the phone,
her doctor said *possible abnormality*

and she has studied that part of her body
each night since,
pulling her fibrous D-cup glands
toward her heart to see
her own flank,
the perfect birthmark, dark and raised,
the patch of mottled skin,
even the red spot, the little target
where maybe it hurts a little,
where maybe it *kills*;
she has been grinding her teeth.
These new views are taken
on a day still shrugging off winter,
a bright day,
but she feels mowed down,
already harvested.
The x-rays are quick
but her neck cramps
from the way the technician twists her,
turns her from the ribs
and shoulder joint, then walks away
to push the button,
while the mass of her lies defeated,
and she, perspiring a little
like a lady,
learns how to pray.

Another Word for Chemo
(for Kevin Stone)

After tilting into Houston
where he drops his splendid feathers
on the Rothko Chapel and the nurses' station,
the blue-winged one opens the road map of cardinal points
and locates another destination;
he considers heading home.

In Santa Fe, he washes his wounds from a spot
at the pillow-edge of juniper trees, his chest swelling
with each fortnight supply of sacred song.

Every day the blue-winged one begins
with what is left. Climbing up in his natty suit
of remaining feathers
to the tops of the piñons, he blinks,

his beak, sprinkled with sunlight, but sore.
He practices drawing precise circles
of strength on the gentle wind.
Stars travel side to side as he slurps the air,
his ledger of days now glittering with extras.

The blue-winged one listens
to the music bustling about on the breeze,
and how the sequence of tones never changes direction.
He spreads his wings a little further,
bathing his tired body in the fresh desert air,
admiring each perfect sparrow and finch that passes.

This is my life, he says, with just the smallest chirp,
as he brings himself into focus on the unstructured flight,
always remembering where he needs to land.

Three

Dividing Lines

You don't have to understand the whole story.
I won't explain it.

In 1947, Jackson Pollock began his drip paintings.
Barnett Newman pulled long zips down large canvases,
lines hurrying into shape. Agnes Martin drew straight lines that shook.

I want to tell you everything.
That he will slip beyond his daily life, licking wine and gin
with abandon, hoarding stability in boxes around his house.
That she will become terrified of herself and her briny mess of openings.
That the weeks will go faster than the minutes.

But this is one day, the day the dividing line
first started being drawn, the day the edges splattered.
She sits at the table; silence bleeds, plops, distorts.

There is tomorrow.
She orders a glass of it, leaves her lips on the rim.

All Day She Wrote

All day she wrote fragrant notes sticky as caramel.
Even as she slept, she did not resist the idle thrumming
of red words. She dreamt slowly and woke
twisted in sheets of flat afternoon sun. Her truth
was bruised. She knew the nature of things,
that his lungs were almost always wet with the slow
tapestry of gin, pulsing dots of liquid woven
into each repeated glass. She watched herself move
in a spiral, her insides round and mirrored as
what she had managed to reflect. She talked to others,
even laughed, ignored the gluey resin that collected
like sap between her legs. It wouldn't do to mention it.

He was headed someplace whole and specific
but he had limited storage space for the reasons why
he'd never get there. The distance between them
had grown into a grid of panic. She whispered to god
and the ceiling about strength, then said yes
when he returned. The answer stretched like spandex
until her flesh became elastic with its foolish shadows.
He trailed his hand lightly over the moss of her body,
tattooing her with need. She climbed over
into betrayal, held herself from her brief rejoicing.

The Blue Noise

Anything he did, the way he laughed, or held his glass
between fat fingers,

she added this to herself,
folding each detail like a sum into her pliant flesh.

Tell me, he'd say, leaning back
in the wooden chair. So she'd start in

with the oranges she'd bought – 10 for a dollar,
and the stop at the library to return her books.
Everything came just before and just after him.

Her life swelled, fruitful and happy,
around each meeting, each one stacked on the next.
Precarious little boxes of chances.

But one day he said *no.*
At that moment, the waiter brought her a menu. Her throat burned
as if she had scraped it on something sharp.

Her tears were intersecting vectors she swallowed
so he wouldn't hear the blue noise
of her sudden breaking.

She studied him then, how each breath wrapped up in itself,
the way his eyes closed and the veins of his nose blued. How he called her
sweetie and turned away.

She drove home then, drenched in a cycle of memories.
She pushed her shoulder into the comforting space
between her husband's shoulders.
Put her wet face on his clean,
quiet shirt.

Fluttering Her Hallelujah Hands

She rearranges his voice into chords,
into a strange jazz she is willing to hear,
a form of organization that takes courage
and leaves her with what is only musical
for a time. The room builds up an energy,
not from the sound of him but from the
collapsing space, the walls pushing in
and her hoarse voice falling, clunking
onto the ground without her, her lips
chapping and the glue wearing thin;
he zigzags into her again but she isn't
listening. She adores the black song
on her radio instead, the saxophone hip-
dancing onto the counter between them,
the babble of nuance moving through pipes
and valves, the rhythm of lopsided feeling.
She is listening to that, and to the halves
of herself binding together into the noise
of the room, and yes, she is willing to
hear his faraway words with her warrior
heart, willing to let him choose her
for his fantasy, to be his bottle of song,
his break from the bruised sunset he sees
from his window. She understands that
what has happened inside her is not
bitter or broken, but that the elastic
of her longing has grown dry and
there is music enough without him.

A Short Version of the Year

he swallowed the birds three dozen years ago washed away
the noise of wonder with swallows sunk inside a bottle an empty
man gnawing on himself his life turning dark if he said a word

her vision is miniature a moment at a round table the yawning
perfume of want the vantage of being inside a marble speckled
with miracles in the glow of solitary attention the sounds

they create when their tongues move a strange religion
about to tarnish her eyes will sleep hard she will cavort with her tears
the grease and grit of memory she is all air ambushed by five different

melodies of sorrow but sound is loyal a philosophical argument that wins
each Monday the angles of Monk merging into a möbius of Bird
and the punishing pinch of bop each note like kisses spinning

in her ears then receding the news is always on her skin
in flames etching hope into the atonal sounds of sin unbroken
minutes pouring into her even now in sleep liquid missing in a missing cup

Getting to the End and Starting Over

Stuck in the parentheses of sleep and sadness, in the
Blackest sentence of feeling

I am of two kinds at once swaddled and now exiled.
Incomplete from myself alone,

A comma between two indistinct thoughts,
An intimate whine that gathered for months on the page. I am

Clause envying transition, a statement spurned by another
Ink-black and cursive. When I head down again

In the hooks and clasps
Of ruthless compound thought,

Virginia sends success tips by email:
I am listing five ecstatic events she writes

From San Rafael, where mornings hunch quietly, the punctuation
Of fog disheveled by a wet wind.

When I crouch into the shadows of error and shame
And rise empty-handed

She reminds me to consider each absolute,
Each interjection. *I am proud* she says

of the moments I unraveled. Her words pull open
The little parts of me,

Combing and softening each twisted line,
Helping me to locate each lost link,

Any wily
Exclamatory flare.

Keep doing what you're doing she writes,
Rolling me gently forward in my search.

Joy is a series of necessary marks,
All white space and targets.

Crying

Drop twelve tears
on a tin plate and listen to the banging.

Eat the tears alone
with knife and spoon.

(Always have manners,
even when you are only half living.)

Then eat the mountain as it rises
over the quiet village.

Chew up the blanched blue lake
and swallow the bulbous moon.

When you are sitting in a cloud,
hungry for hope,

enjoy the exertion of exercising your heart.
Hold the rain on your face.

The rapid release of brief woes
is expedient,

a small compensation
for the naked places you've slept.

A Precise Small Thing

I didn't know I would run out of time to memorize
your voice. After three days trying, I just now remember
the name of a trombonist I heard three years ago,
and you have been missing 3,322 days.

Dad laughed when I asked for the recording of you
saying *no one is home right now* with your wine-sopped,
grass-pure voice. I can't remember it at all, that voice.

Not the strange wide way you had of stretching Ws
or the laugh that started from a precise small thing
and rolled on and on, expanding into time
we didn't realize was ending.

Or the way you called to us, your voice becoming
a near shriek in the almost dark, our names as large as puppets
expected to move back into that box of home again.

Or how you said *Dad.* Just that one word.
How you cried at the supper table some nights,
your voice turning into salt and red breath.

How you moaned gently. How your voice in my hands
expired into something I could no longer hear,
something smaller than atoms.

How I Dream My Mother in Someone Else

Each version of precision is evanescent.
Every night I watch someone die.

In my dream last night, a terrier followed me
and I turned away. A woman put on shoes,
then took them off. A man tied up his hair.

I knew the point they faded, the swell and crust
of each last breath.

The man was feverish; his blue back slumped
under my hand.

I can trace the whisper of my lips
on his forehead, his face scrubbed of color.
In my sleep he shuddered and was gone.

I hold on to my tight grief. The terrier barks.
In my dream the shoes are empty. Every night
it is something else.

The cavern of sleep closes in,
then morning shovels it out for me to study.

It is on waking that I cry, my face wet without her.

What Remains

Days pass
and all the knotted sounds
are red as your fingers
twisting her dry collection
of missing bones;
your long stretch of face
knitted to her forgotten one;
her diminished memory,
sneakered and lanky;
her sweater deep as bottled wine,
crimson as the family convertible
brimming with B-side songs
on bulky eight-track tapes;
and now you know
the best part of the music
is missing, blurred
from its wine-sweet optimism
until everything you remember
is only buried
in the occasional misplaced tune
from that musical
where your brother tap danced
down carpeted red stairs,
and Dorothy keeps singing
as the house turns circles
and the crows cry
in the open field of your new life
yielding a hundred blank
memories formed without her,
as you grow,
persistent but clumsy,
into your bones.

Mt. Eden

On the first day back, we cross the bridge;
drive through trees lucent with autumn. Dad parks

the white car on a hill and we walk the green slope
past the babies. He points out my mother's neighbors.

It rains on my mother,
a pink mist, softer

than the last time I stood here; the sky is glaucous,
blurry

with all these spirits, the grass neatly trimmed.
A walnut shell and black river rock sit side by side

on the wet marble;
it's like someone placed a period after a period,

offered a tight collection of enclosed nature for the journey
of the sentence. My father bends

and reads aloud, his hairy fingers moving slowly
over the cut letters of the wet stone,

reciting dates and Torah verse
like a blind man touching lines and space for answers.

Two days later, my brother and I return
in his SUV; as we drive, we are listening

to Laurie Anderson's
word world and the politics of voice.

He is never sure how to get where we need to be.
His cell phone rings, and I expect my mother

to tell us which way to turn,
but my brother talks to someone else. I have ash on my hand

and my heart hurts. We are the only guests
at the cemetery, transposing

departure and separation. The babies whimper;
reason comes slowly.

My brother lies on the lawn
where my mother's body is, where the bones remain

lined up neatly, her wrists and skull,
femur and pelvis. Dirt holds her memory in place.

He crosses his strong arms behind his head
and relaxes, looking straight up

into a glistening sun. That night I hear on the radio
that elephants, too, visit the bones of their loved ones.

Charo and the Colors of Coping

Charo shows up in my studio.
I am mixing colors but I look up because I don't expect her.
In her thick accent, she tells me she misses her whole name:
María Rosario Pilar Martínez Molina Moquiere de les Esperades
Santa Ana Romanguera y de la Najosa Rasten.
She jiggles her bosom up and down.
I continue painting, even though I don't paint.
I can't find the right colors, or something to say.
Outside, the apple tree grows leaves and drops them.
Mom is dead but I have been given an extra day with her.
We sit on the couch and watch Chico and the Man.
Charo does her cuchi-cuchi down the stairs, but I am watching Chico grin.
Mom doesn't tell me that Chico pulled a trigger on himself.
I am a girl in the middle of my illuminations.
When my mother's not looking, I touch the flat places where my nipples are.
Everything I know I learn from sitcoms:
Laverne De Fazio and Edith Bunker, Laura Ingalls and Wonder Woman.
My life skills are limited.
I roll Dad's 200 black socks together into furry blobs while the TV is on.
Charo is getting annoyed.

She wants this to be about her, so she gets out her guitar.
She plays one of Segovia's Estudios.
She tosses her hair into the living room and wriggles those pillowy tits.
She shuffles her tiny sequined dress.
Ach-ren't we chaving a goood tyme? Charo says carefully.
A horse galumphs in her throat.
A frog belches.
She laughs.
Mom and I watch eight episodes of The Love Boat to make Charo happy.
Charo does her cuchi-cuchi on the ship's prow.
The captain smiles.
She addresses her body to wherever they're sailing this week.
And the water continues curving into waves.
Afterwards, we go out for ice cream.
My mother orders a triple chocolate sundae with fudge sauce.
She always gets the same thing.
Charo orders a vanilla cone with pink sprinkles.
When we're done licking and slurping, I go back to my studio.
I turn our laughter between my palms and paint it.
Mom is about to disappear again, but I think I've finally gotten it right.
I find the colors by mixing dewy brights with black.

When He Asks about Her Dreams

No hours, no messenger,
no morning until the blue runs out
and there is no front
and the back recedes into a prism of emptiness.

She walks down the glass steps, past hundreds of shoes.
This repetition of breath is nearly too much.
Each step in, each step down
her staircase of vibrant colors –

reeling in the cinema of sleep.
She holds thirteen variations in her eyes,
those confused peeling memories
all out of proportion.

(How about the blazing dollhouse
and the doctor's ruined jacket? Do they mean something?)

She always tilts forward into the tread of it,
the long pull of dreams.
One more time. Again, she says.

Why should she unfold herself into day
when the entire world is perfectly contained
in one large room of her mind?

What she does in the dark, it's a story,
whole, and she is not surprised
by the mysterious symbols, the many layers of shoes.

She had never been in a place where the moon blooms,
or bridges lead to mirrors,
where the sky rains colored feathers and we don't get wet.

Tell me where you are, he says,
as morning nudges in to claim her.

The sweet soupy moments are leaving her body.
She opens her eyes, peeling through layers, climbing up slowly
in her bare feet, step by step
into the fading light of memory.

56

This Business of Wisdom

Eddie died when he was no longer Ovadia.
Bill wore a boater hat to China.
Stan explains the profit gained by selling someone's car.

Jen is practically on her own, ignoring her husband's fixed gaze,
– and once a day
she roller skates, caressing the flat street of silence.

Aunt M. complains the gun is not tiny.
I hear her gulp and scowl.

Lou writes from a truck, gazing
a route through the Midwest. The flimsy sound of his headlights

distracts me. I know a man and a woman named Dallas.
Both are rumpled.

Eddie died and I wrote to Mira. *Mira* means look.
Look sometimes means look away.

At my mother's funeral, a friend looked at me and
called me by *her* name instead of mine.
The short excursion of memory tormented me.

How old was I the night soccer became fingers on my skin? How old when.
I apologized for the party.

I need to buy
a handful of yellow pear tomatoes.

He says I'll be jealous. I've been to Ireland.

The day Eddie died.

The day after. Nothing special.
A lemonade cup. A day when the sun poised on the horizon.

How the Sun Opens Us, Even in Winter

Singed

Walking along the upper tier, I turn a corner
and pass above a perfect swelling gleam;
one hundred sorority girls
with long blonde hair,
talking at once, a continuous fierce wave,
the sway of their voices stronger and more illuminated
than any other sound in my world.
I am drifting this day and – lucky,
move into the rays of that single shaft of ecstatic light,
the elemental pitch of their tongues rising up, blistering
and piercing even the floor on which I stand.
I abandon any destination,
gaze straight down at the sparkling blaze,
watch as they move, luminous and golden,
through the cold open room,
scattering and radiating light so it glitters and hums
in a corona of energy.
I love those women then – all of them at once.
So yellow they are, so tempting,
the pollen of their voices distracting,
so intense it steals over the body,
almost more than I can bear,
but I cannot turn away. Looking, looking –
until my eyes burn.

The Sun Blur

One afternoon, my nephew and I
walk the concrete path around his house.
He keeps rushing ahead, quickening,
his appetite for himself unending.
Surprised, the boy of four,
that the sun walks over us
and that we always return back to it.
He loves the heavy cloud his shadow casts,

and I do too. The vague bluster,
the dark smear of him on sidewalk,
the stretched body of his small form becoming
and disappearing again in migrant light.
There is too much excitement
and he cannot find enough.
We hurry forward to look again,
to see how it is done,
how light is slurped up by darkness.

Sunrise on My Birthday

Chilled, I stand inside a shadow,
puffed and solitary,
and as I want the cold to stop, the snow descends,
floating and rippling around in a canopy,
then sleeping gently on the ground,
turning the outdoors into a platter
with a wide debonair sky.
And the sun, a juicy segment of orange,
climbs slowly up the nearby mountain,
a lustrous brandy-tinted slice of hope.

Cyclamen

After so many frigid days,
the cyclamen have begun unscrolling
their pink plumes again,
each thin plate of soft silk lifting into the light,
proud and long-limbed,
each blushing petal rising higher,
confident as it sweeps the air.
Winter is a cycle of damnation and beauty,
a hundred days to stumble and hide.
My body leans into the fringe of warmth
and lingers, asks for nothing more.
Even the darkest months make sense,
the steady flaring of empty days.
Even these I am learning to embrace.

Slow

Eyes open, legs splayed in the powdery dirt,
she likes the cool of it, the dynamic surge
of just belonging to a place like this,
brown and barren and slow as rust.

She digs deeper with her toes and hums.
When the sun crests the kitchen window,
she catches fragments of light on her thumb
and drags her hand across her chin –
like buttercups.

This will be the year the piñons die,
the year the tamarisks stretch inches to the core,
the year she goes away
– and then returns
to find the worms still multiplying.

Maybe there is no final resolution,
yesterday is how it will be again tomorrow.
The earth will slowly crust into tenacious particles,
stillness cradled inside like a newborn.

Raised in New York, **LAUREN CAMP** has lived in a rural village south of Santa Fe, New Mexico since 1994. She spends part of each week writing, producing and broadcasting "Audio Saucepan," an hour of eclectic music and words, for KSFR-FM Public Radio.

She is also an accomplished visual artist – creating fiber portraits, sculptures and mixed-media work. Her series, "The Fabric of Jazz," was exhibited in ten museums in the U.S. over a four-year period. Many of her works have been commissioned, collected and exhibited by hospitals, museums, cultural centers, U.S. embassies, and other public places.

To learn more, visit www.laurencamp.com.

This is Lauren's first book.